His Touch

His Touch

*A Study of Holiness Teaching
in the
Miracles of Jesus*

**by
Peter W. Gentry**

BEACON HILL PRESS OF KANSAS CITY
Kansas City, Missouri

ISBN: 0-8341-0665-5

Dedication

Contents

Preface

It will doubtless be generally agreed that all teaching and experience of the Spirit-filled life must take us back to the example of the Apostolic Church as described in the New Testament. Christian holiness realised by faith as a recognisable work of grace subsequent to the new birth is not an innovation, nor is it an isolated spiritual fad or emotional crisis. It is simply the recovery of normal, honest Christianity as begun in the second chapter of Acts on the Day of Pentecost. It is the personal experience of what the Saviour made possible for all believers by His atonement and resurrection.

Christ himself is, of course, the greatest exemplar of the faith that bears His name. Christians are such because they have become partakers of His risen life, and they are predestined to be like Him in moral and spiritual character (Rom. 8:29). His life on earth is therefore the blueprint for ours. Recognising that our Lord was capable, by virtue of His deity, of actions impossible to us on a purely human plane, it is yet true that He "who went about doing good" (Acts 10:38) left us an example, that we should follow His steps (1 Pet. 2:21). The immediate context of those steps is that they led to Calvary, where He, the sinless One, bore our sin that we might live unto righteousness. We are called to follow those steps and be spiritually crucified with Christ, then raised into newness of life in Him, so that He might thus indwell us and continue through our lives the life that He lived on earth as a man.

Those steps from His home at Nazareth to the hill of Calvary were steps of miracle. Before He left the little band of disciples gathered in the Upper Room for that last Passover supper, Jesus spoke to them about the Holy Spirit who would come to be with them as He had himself been with them all that time. He prayed with them that they might be truly sanctified by the Spirit so that He could send them into the world fully united in Him and with the Father. He had said to them, "He that believeth on me, the works that I do shall he do also; and greater works than these shall he do" (John 14:12). Jesus intended His miracles to be continued in the lives of the sanctified, and He put no limit to them.

The miracles wrought in and through the Early Church did not, alas, continue into the postapostolic age, though a marked resumption of them is happily being seen in these days. We can therefore take the recorded miracles of the Lord Jesus and the evident purpose in His mind that they should have direct relevance to the lives of His people, and prayerfully relate them to our present Christian life and experience. As we do this, may it be that our hearts shall be challenged and that we shall seek such an utter abandonment to the Holy Ghost as will transform our discipleship and give us power with God and with men. His touch represents the miracle of holiness in us.

I send forth these few devotional studies in the hope and prayer that the truth that has so blessed my own soul may be made an even greater blessing to those who read them.

Peter W. Gentry

Weston-super-Mare,
England

1

His Touch and Sin

Nothing matters more in heaven or on earth than the glory of the Lord Jesus Christ. It is central in creation, in history, in redemption, and in experience.

When the time came for His glory to be revealed by miracle in the midst of earthly men, that moment enabled Him to identify its true purpose—nothing less than the total transformation of mankind. In order to achieve that end, He had come as Mary's Son to deal radically with sin. He may not have chosen the wedding feast at Cana as either the time or the place for this unveiling, though His mother left Him in an awkward position by causing the servants to look expectantly to Him for the needed wine. After reproving her, the Lord turned to the vessels of purification and changed their contents from water into wine (John 2:1-11).

John declared of the Son of God that "he . . . came by water and blood" (1 John 5:6) and that to this the Spirit bears witness. At the last Passover supper with His disciples, Jesus held a cup of red wine and said, "This is my blood of the new [covenant], which is shed for many for the remission of sins" (Matt. 26:28). The signifying of water as natural birth and blood as divine redemption provides an insight into the real significance of His first miracle, and indeed of all those that followed. He came to lead men and women through purification of heart and life from the natural to the spiritual, from defilement to discipleship.

One of the finest of that sturdy breed of Christians, the early Cornish Methodists, was William Carvosso. An ignorant, hard-drinking fisherman from Mousehole, he was wonderfully converted; and although no preacher like Billy Bray, he became a personal soul-winner of great renown throughout the Duchy. When he was seeking holiness, he attended a cottage meeting and says that just as he entered the room, he sensed a truly heavenly atmosphere and thought to himself, I shall have the blessing now. Immediately, the Lord responded by His Spirit and gave Carvosso the witness that the work was done. He wrote, "I cried out, 'This is what I wanted. I have now got a new heart.' I was emptied of self and sin, and filled with God."

Yes, an empty waterpot into a vessel brimming with the royal wine of the Kingdom—that is exactly the change that our wonderful Saviour wants to accomplish in our lives. To do so, He must deal with the sore point of sin.

This is such a fearful reality that, in the New Testament accounts of our Lord's miracles, we find sin illustrated in no less than five different ways, and in each situation He confronted the problem and vanquished it. Let us take a look at each of them.

1. *Leprosy* takes the lead. Perhaps it may be significant that the first healing miracle detailed in the first Gospel concerns a leper (Matt. 8:2-4). Sin separates the soul from

God just as totally as leprosy isolates the sufferer from his fellowmen. It pollutes and disfigures the soul like the disease infests and distorts the flesh. Both are unalterably fatal in the natural course.

Nothing is more appealingly beautiful in all the Scriptures than the word picture of the Saviour unhesitatingly putting out His hand and touching the hideous form of this pathetic man who had shuffled up to Him and, with undeniable faith, knelt to seek His help. How gloriously effective was the remedy! "I will; be thou clean"; and he was! It was not the start of a long process of recovery; it was an instant deliverance. Just so, the soul cannot grow clean, neither is it purified by process. It is either clean or defiled; and when the Saviour touches its infection in response to our yielded trust in Him, it is cleansed at once. Then, as "we walk in the light" with Him, "the blood of Jesus Christ his Son cleanseth us from all sin" (1 John 1:7). Hallelujah! What a Saviour!

2. Sin also is illustrated by a *fever*, to which again it has many similarities. A person in a high fever is nearly always delirious; the mind is stupefied, bemused, disordered. Sin also works like that, as the apostle Paul knew to his painful recollection when he declared, "Sin . . . deceived me, and . . . slew me" (Rom. 7:11). It clothes itself with false colours so as to make one believe it is quite acceptable, even sometimes virtuous; it beguiles the sensitive conscience into deciding that it should learn to be reasonable. Fever is mental chaos. All sorts of weird and fantastic images dance about in the mind until it cries out some incoherent words or moans a meaningless protest. Isaiah truly diagnosed the fever of sin when he said, "The whole head is sick, and the whole heart faint" (1:5).

Again, there is very little that can be done to end or cure a fever. Modern medication certainly helps to bring it down; but more often than not, it is a case of watching and waiting while it runs its course. It is very much like that with the plague of the heart. It can to some extent be controlled by prayer and self-discipline, and there is always the hope of better things; but we can never overcome it. Always it will break out somewhere, like a depressed balloon. The quick-tempered will be sure to explode, the susceptible will be caught off guard, persistent pressure ultimately wins the day, and the fences go down. How many of us know this only too well!

When steam locomotives were first introduced into one area of the world, a local engineer, alarmed at the sudden blast of steam from the safety valve, tied the valve down to stop the deafening noise; as a result, the boiler blew up, killing both him and his fireman. The steam just had to escape, and trying to stop it only made worse havoc in the end. In the same way, you cannot suppress sin.

Peter's mother-in-law was suffering from a fever. Luke, with the physician's expert eye, called it "a great fever" (4:38-39). But this, too, responded at once to the Master's touch, and the fever left her. Not in any form can sin survive His touch. He has the complete answer to the problem.

3. A further illustration is *paralysis*. In this case, the sufferer did not even need His touch; His word was enough.

> *Thy touch has still its ancient power;*
> *No word from Thee can fruitless fall.*

When the paralysed man was carried on a stretcher by his four friends to the house where Jesus was ministering and lowered to His feet through the opened roof, He only needed to say to him, "Son, be of good cheer; thy sins be forgiven thee" (Matt. 9:2; cf. vv. 1-8). The immediate flurry of puzzled conversation that these words produced evidently deterred the man from acting upon them; but after affirming to those present His rightful authority to forgive sins, the Lord bade him arise, take up his couch, and walk, which he did to the astonishment of all.

It is a wise doctor who will sometimes say to a patient in his consulting room, "You know, it is really a minister you need to see rather than me." The spiritual stress brought on by unconfessed or unforgiven sin will react on the nervous system and affect the physical health in consequence. "For this cause," wrote Paul to the Corinthians concerning partaking of the Lord's Supper while harboring unconfessed sin, "many are weak and sickly among you, and many sleep" (1 Cor. 11:30). The tension of guilt is disastrous to health, and the real need is not a medical cure but getting right with God. How many Christians, even, would have to admit that spiritual defeat has laid them low and paralysed their witness? How good it is to know that "if we confess our sins, he is faithful and just to forgive us our sins, and to cleanse us from all unrighteousness" (1 John 1:9).

4. *Bondage* is another picture of what sin can do. Near where I lived as a boy in suburban London, there used to be a junction where two streetcar lines diverged. The switch was operated by an old man who pulled a lever at the curbside. He used to sit on an orange box and when a car came along, he would get up and pull over the big iron lever, directing the car to its proper destination. His back was so bent that it was only when he pulled the lever towards him and held on to it as the car passed over the switch that he ever saw straight ahead; at all other times his gaze could be fixed only groundwards.

I often think of that dear old man when I read the story of the healing of the woman with curvature of the spine whom Jesus restored in the synagogue one Sabbath day (Luke 13:10-17). Pulling the lever at least helped him to get upright for a minute or two, but it did nothing to straighten his back. But Christ's hands could straighten the woman's back permanently after 18 years of being bound by this disease. The Lord referred to her as "a daughter of Abraham"; and in John 8:36, where He was disputing with those who prided themselves on their descent from the patriarch of faith, He declared, "If the Son therefore shall make you free, ye shall be free indeed."

The law of sin in our members keeps us bent spiritually just as the spinal disease kept this poor woman doubled up. One of the New Testament Greek words for sin (*adikia*) literally means "crookedness"; and another (*hamartia*) denotes "missing the mark." The connection is obvious; how can you possibly hit the target if you cannot even look straight at it? Christ gives us power to be inwardly unbound and lifted up to moral and spiritual straightness, to level and clear vision of His way and will, and to the healthy exercise of a totally renewed life. "But now being made free [literally, 'unhitched'] from sin, and become servants to God, ye have your fruit unto holiness, and the end everlasting life" (Rom. 6:22).

5. It is perhaps in the symbol of *darkness* that sin assumes its most austere and frightening form. It is nature's night. Second only to lack of love, loss of light is man's greatest predicament. Christ is "the true Light, which lighteth every man that cometh into the world" (John 1:9); which is to say that everyone, despite the Fall, is capable of salvation by responding to the truth of the gospel, such is the greatness of God's love. But the sin nature, left to itself, finally obliterates that light, and all that is left is darkness. As Paul put it, speaking of the unregenerate, "Their foolish heart was darkened" (Rom. 1:21). If there is a chink of that light of prevenient grace left in us, it will be enough to show us how dark everything else is inside and set us longing for more light. George Fox, the pioneer Quaker, wrote to Elizabeth Claypole, Cromwell's

daughter, who was then a seeker, "The same light that shows you your sin will show you your Saviour."

When Jesus saw the beggar who was born blind, He spoke of the night that was coming and proceeded to lead him out of his natural darkness into the light of a brand-new life (John 9:1-7). The Pharisees tried to argue him out of this wonderful experience by branding Christ as a sinner. His reply to them is full of meaning: "Whether he be a sinner or no, I know not: one thing I know, that, whereas I was blind, now I see" (v. 25). This man had received more than eyesight; one feels he had also come to see himself for the first time.

How was it wrought, this beautiful miracle? The Saviour anointed the blind man's eyes with moist clay and instructed him to go and wash in the Pool of Siloam. Could this be said to illustrate "the washing of regeneration, and renewing of the Holy Ghost" (Titus 3:5)? Surely the typography would not be unfitting. Jesus is the Light of the World, and He can deal with sin as light deals with darkness—by total exclusion. While we abide in His light, there is no room for lingering shadows.

His touch upon sin, then, is one that cleanses, calms, forgives, releases, and illuminates the soul. The way to prove that is to come to Him by commitment and faith, and then the whole pattern of God's grace can be experienced. In the village church at Norbury in Cheshire, there is a stained-glass window bearing the text "For by one offering he hath perfected for ever them that are sanctified" (Heb. 10:14). Looked at from the outside, it is just dark-coloured glass, unreadable and unattractive; but from inside the sanctuary the same window with the light shining through shows its loveliness plainly for all to see—and so does its message shine.

17

We may "enter into the holiest by the blood of Jesus. . ... Let us draw near . . . in full assurance of faith" (Heb. 10:19, 22).

2

His Touch and Self

Somewhere in the hazy borderlands between the physical and the spiritual makeup of mankind, there dwells the mysterious entity we call "self." For all its lack of definition, it is the real you and the real me. It is at the same time commanding and elusive. It is not so totally moral as the heart and will, where our motives, desires, and decisions are worked out; neither is it nonmoral in the same way as the fibres of the body and nervous system. Yet the self-life is not truly amoral, for it is capable of response to the claims of authority. Paul's excruciating wretchedness in Rom. 7:24 resulted from the fact that his mind and his body each wanted to act in its own way, and his true self was consequently distracted and tortured. It was only when the Holy Spirit set him inwardly free that his self-life settled down to a happy integration in Christ.

It has often been said by its critics that the Bible knows nothing of modern psychology. Certainly it is unacquainted with much of its verbiage, and for this we must be thankful. Perhaps in some ways the penmen of Scripture saw only the blacks and the whites and little of the grey areas; that much may be fair comment. In the world of Bible times (and ours) the black was very black and the white all the more brilliant by contrast. But the Lord Jesus Christ was a superb worker in the grey areas. It was said of Him that "he knew what was in man" (John 2:25), and He saw not only what people did but understood why they acted as they did.

To believers who are seriously concerned with the life of spiritual fulness and victory, the self-life poses a real problem. The struggles of the saints are waged in this arena. There are so many things we would like to be and to do in fulfilment of Christian ideals that somehow we do not manage to achieve. Though our faith in God and love for Christ are sincere and complete so far as we know, there is a blockage of power to get us where we feel we need to be. Conversely, we often find ourselves responding to urges that seem to be so much a part of our nature, sanctified as we believe it to be, yet are difficult to reconcile with the will of God or the mind of the Spirit. To quote Paul again, "To will is present with me; but how to perform . . . I find not" (Rom. 7:18).

These tensions are especially keen when one is seeking to live for Christ in a world that revels in the philosophy of "Be yourself" and "Do your own thing." Such questions arise as, Is it right to want to succeed and achieve one's ambitions when God's Word says, "He must increase, but I must decrease" (John 3:30)? What is sinful and what is simply human? If I believe that "with God all things are possible" (Matt. 19:26), why is it that I just cannot seem to bring myself to do certain things such as speak in public or pray aloud? How far am I justified in making allowances for my own peculiar attitudes when I know they cause pain or problems to others but do not seem to me to be wrong? Unredeemed society will simply accept that I am what I am and react accordingly, but in the family of God there are different standards of action and reaction; so can I really be myself without failing the Lord? Can my likeness and Christlikeness ever identify with each other?

A study of other miracles, in which the Saviour dealt so wonderfully with real people and real situations, might help us over some of these difficulties. Let us see.

Personality

We are meant to be whole people. The entire personality is precious because, even yet, it carries the image of God; it is eternal, sacred, and intended to glorify man's Maker. Whatever the saintly Quaker, Thomas Kelly, meant when he spoke of Christians needing to be "unselfed," it certainly was not that personality should be destroyed. It cannot be. It is the body of sin that must suffer this well-merited fate. Personality needs to be sublimated to the divine purpose and fitted for its final destiny in the kingdom of heaven.

If personality is to attain its God-given role in the Christian life, it must be united and undivided. This fact is summed up in David's prayer, "Unite my heart to fear thy name" (Ps. 86:11). When the entirely healed personality is brought under the rule of the Spirit, discipleship and service will be effective and satisfying. While there is internal conflict between self-will and God's will, our lives will be ineffectual and spiritually dwarfed. "The flesh lusteth against the Spirit, and the Spirit against the flesh: and these are contrary the one to the other: so that ye cannot do the things that ye would" (Gal. 5:17). That is not to be understood as the Christian norm, but it was the Galatians' experience, and Paul roundly condemned it. There was a better way.

The Master one day healed a blind and dumb man

who was brought to Him. This naturally caused quite a stir; and the sullen attitude of the Pharisees boiled over in the angry and very stupid accusation, "This fellow doth not cast out devils, but by Beelzebub the prince of the devils" (Matt. 12:24; cf. vv. 22-30). Unmerited scorn is always pathetic; it never makes even simple sense. A moment's thought would show that two like forces working against each other would be mutually ruinous. Like equal figures in a fraction, they would cancel out each other in effectiveness. The poor man who had been so wondrously released from Satan's grip had been set free only by One stronger than the enemy, just as the strong man in the mini-parable that followed was overpowered and his house plundered by one of superior strength. If Christ's power over evil was effective, it was because His power was of God.

In other words, power is only released when undivided forces are used. Satan kept his prisoner by sheer malignity. Jesus freed him by total love. The spiritual lesson in this is apparent. If our personality is united in Christ, our warfare against the enemy will be victorious. A war on two fronts is nearly always unsuccessful. When the personality is completely yielded to the love of God and kept under the discipline of the Holy Spirit, its total self can find fulfilment. The parts of our makeup that God cannot use, He will change; the parts that He can use, He will. If I am His all the way, all of me will respond to His touch and develop in grace.

We must not think, however, that the Saviour deals with everyone in such a way as to produce a stereotyped monotony. The human soul is created with the same divine flair for variety and sensitivity as are all His works. Hence it follows that He deals with us as individuals, taking due account of the value of personality with its endless light and shade and its mysterious bundle of latent possibilities. Even though grace has its definitive experiences of conversion and sanctification, the Lord will come to us before, between, and beyond these crises and treat us according to our different personal characteristics. One soul may open to Christ as naturally as a flower to the sun; another may need a veritable earthquake to bring conviction and surrender. What matters is not the "how" but the result.

It is the individualness of His touch that means so much, as shown so graphically in the case of the deaf mute whom Jesus healed by two touches—one to his ears, the other to his mouth (Mark 7:31-37). His word alone could have wrought the miracle; or a single touch, as in so many others, could have sufficed. But no! The Saviour bestowed an individual touch to each area of need, and both were restored to normal function. The onlookers on that occasion exclaimed, "He hath done all things well." Indeed, He has!

Mind

All-important to any consideration of the self-life is the exercise of the imagination. Much Christian living that is devotedly sound and true to scriptural values suffers from being unimaginative. Its very rigidity is its undoing when confronted with something a little out of the ordinary. Its outlook has been fixed so long in one direction that it cannot see in any other. This immediately raises the question of how far the mind influences our inner life.

To the ancients, mind and heart were very closely related. "As [a man] thinketh in his heart, so is he," runs the proverb (Prov. 23:7). Our volitional powers are controlled by our mental images. These are capable of enormous good or incalculable harm. One of the extraordinary factors of the human mind is its ability to conceive both beauty and blight. The prophet Ezekiel described the chambers of imagery in which the leaders of Israel hung upon the walls of their minds all manner of unclean and idolatrous things (Ezek. 8:7-12), and these were religious people. Like it or not, we live according to the pictures we form as the result of our contact with truth, environment, and culture. The vital point, then, is the recovery of the mind to clear thinking and loving imagination. Can this be done? What of the subconscious and even the unconscious thoughts which nevertheless play their part in decision making and attitude forming?

The hymn writer Charlotte Elliott's words, "Sight, riches, healing of the mind," affirm what the New Testament abundantly reveals, that the total range of Christ's healing power includes the mind of man no less than the body. His effect on wrong thinking is, of course, demonstrated by His words rather than in the miracles insofar as recorded reaction conveys it to us. Mental therapy taking place under the impact of His teaching comes through, for example, in the case of the lawyer who began (as lawyers often do) by justifying himself; but then he listened to the parable about neighbourly love and recognised in the end where his attitude had been so wrong (Luke 10:25-37). And it shows in the scribe, probably no less prone to that legal failing for all his loquacious ways, whom Jesus commended as being "not far from the kingdom of God" (Mark 12:34). Some of the peculiar attitudes of the disciples did not seem to change very much until the Holy Spirit came, but the transformation was wonderful after then; and this is, after all, how it will be effected in us as the Spirit reveals the Saviour and applies His words to our minds (see John 16:13-15).

In the healing miracles, we are naturally confronted with extreme cases of mental disturbance resulting from demon possession and, consequently, out of the orbit of the kind of problems known to ordinary people. But the case of Legion, whom the Lord restored to normality in

Gadara, is important to our present study for two reasons. First, because it shows how the powers of imagination can be so distorted, the poor man's regiment of demons seeming to him like a legion of soldiers such as he had probably seen marching down the coast road from Caesarea; and second, because after his meeting with the Saviour, he was found "in his right mind." The evil spirits that stripped and tore him had gone, and so too had the by-product of personality imbalance (Mark 5:1-17; Luke 8:26-36). Christ can not only deliver from sin but also restore the mind to clear, right, and balanced thinking and to that inner poise which is the very essence of a healthy self-life.

Human Appetites

It is no sin to be hungry, feel tired, fall in love, or earn good money. Physical life must certainly not be indulged, but neither should it be denied those things which are proper to its normal satisfaction. The Master's insistence that a would-be disciple must "deny himself" refers to the orientation of life—around Him and not around oneself—rather than the creaturely necessities of living.

Yet there is a question here of proportion and relativity which has proved a snare to many a Christian. The fact is that, sadly, many who confess Christ do not seem to be finding their complete satisfaction in Him. They are continually trying to find new outlets for their increasing leisure time, new spheres of activity, and new enjoyments. Possibly this is because we live in a seething, restless age. So many attractions and diversions are offered in modern life that were unknown a generation or two ago, and people—especially young people—are easily caught up in the general scramble to think of life in terms of the latest model car, the most popular TV programme, and a dream house with every modern luxury to go with it. Money today is not lacking to make these dreams come true in many cases.

Let it not be thought that we are advocating a purely negative outlook towards these good things of life. Indeed, we can praise God that for so many, life has become so much more pleasant with the greater variety and mobility that this mechanised age has brought about; and all these amenities can be held in faithful stewardship by the sanctified Christian and made a blessing to many. But at the same time, there is a danger that with so much within the reach of the average person, many causes of spiritual erosion can arise; and sadly, many of the Lord's people have joined the materialistic merry-go-round. They have not ceased to be Christians—even witnessing ones—but they *have* ceased to be vital, Christ-centered, Spirit-anointed ones because the simplicity of discipleship has been lost to the complicated tempo of modern life.

One cannot help feeling that 20th-century sainthood is sometimes rather feeble compared to that of a century or two ago! Machinery violates meditation. Christian cassettes crowd out Bible study. Programmes replace prayer. Jesus *alone* no longer seems to satisfy the whole person. It is insidious but quite unmistakable.

The miracles of the feeding of the multitudes so clearly illustrate how wonderfully Jesus satisfies the complete human need, and not just at basic level but to repletion (Matt. 14:15-21; 15:32-38). On both occasions, the assembled thousands were filled despite the absence of sufficient natural food for them and the inability of either the disciples or the people to provide any more. It was enough that *He* was there. And yet it was real food that He gave them—bread and fish, the staple diet to which they were accustomed. It was no symbolic or sacramental feast, either; it was a square meal for each one, with enough scraps left over to feed probably several hundreds more.

This, then, provides the answer to the question of how our natural appetites may find their true place in the

Spirit-filled life. Our first priority must be our relationship with the Lord; we will be satisfied with *Him*. Then in stewardship we can receive all the blessings of life which He liberally bestows upon us, not to accumulate them but to use them in Kingdom service. As Wesley said, "Earn all you can; save all you can; give all you can." The best rule for this aspect of the self-life is, "Seek ye first the kingdom of God, and his righteousness; and all these things [e.g., material blessings] will be added unto you" (Matt. 6:33).

Drive

One thing is for sure; the old cry, "Oh, to be nothing," is true neither to Scripture nor human nature. Paul did not see himself that way; his rule for living was, "I can do all things through Christ which strengtheneth me" (Phil. 4:13). "Oh, to be His," yes; but "Oh, to be nothing," never! Christ can be all and I can yet be something in Him. He surely has plans for my life which I can find and follow, and so find fulfilment. The will to venture, attempt, and, if possible, succeed is latent in everyone. Without it, we would be spineless, colourless, robotlike creatures.

Of course, one can drive too fast and too far. To aim at being a good salesman need not involve coveting the top sales executive's job. If I determine that I am going to get to the top of the ladder, come what may, in whatever career I have chosen, I am sure to hurt somebody else and thereby dishonour the Lord. I will also damage my own personality. I would do better to commit my future to Him and go as far and as fast as He leads me to go. But I will be a pale caricature of a person if I do not want to go anywhere.

This motivation that we call drive has therefore to find its pace and its place in discipleship. Let us take Peter as an example. He had plenty of it! Those who rate Peter as a bold man only after Pentecost have not looked at him very closely. Certainly he did not deny his Lord again after then, but that is another matter altogether. He was always an assertive man, the first to speak and to act in everything. When Peter and the other disciples in the boat saw Jesus walking towards them on the surface of the sea, he in his typical way brushed aside his natural fear of so uncanny a sight and called out, "Lord, if it be thou, bid me come unto thee on the water." And He replied, "Come" (Matt. 14:28-29; cf. vv. 22-33). Notice how, despite the wary "if," Peter's drive was encouraged by the Lord and that the eager, confident fisherman actually did walk on the water himself to go to Jesus.

So far, so good. While keeping his eyes on the Lord, Peter was able to exercise his natural drive in a supernatural way. While he set out to reach a divinely approved objective, he could do it; and the Lord enabled him to do it in a way that none of his fellows did. That is surely the way to settle this question of ambition and the urge to achieve; fasten it upon the objective you believe the Lord approves and then keep looking to Him each step of the way. Then you will succeed and nobody else will suffer. Peter got into trouble when he lowered his gaze and realised that it was, after all, a stormy sea he was treading; then, as natural fear took over, he began to sink and was only rescued by the strong arm of the Lord, who gently rebuked him for his lack of faith. Let our trust in Him be total, and let His will be our sole concern; then our drive can not only be safely harnessed but even achieve the unbelievable.

Johann Danneker, the famous sculptor, once refused an emperor's commission to carve a statue of Venus for his palace because he had spent eight years working on a figure of Christ. His artistic senses as well as his spiritual desires had found their true goal in Him, and the other was unthinkable. Yes, it's true—Jesus really satisfies.

Inadequacy

It is a strangely moving picture that is painted for us in John's Gospel (5:1-9) of the pathetic scramble of well-nigh helpless people to be first into the Pool of Bethesda whenever the angel periodically stirred its turgid waters. Imagine trying every time this happened for 38 years and never making it! Yet that was the case with the man whom Jesus healed there. All the others were "impotent folk" and therefore probably in just as bad shape as he, yet he always lost in the attempt.

How true is this of so many of our human inadequacies. One of the prime causes of nervous breakdown, neurosis, and depression is a sense of inadequacy—an in-built conviction that when put to the test, I will fail; that when I have to compete with others for a job, a promotion, or even a date, someone else will surely beat me to it. The opportunity vanishes because I cannot rise up to meet it, knowing I shall miss it anyway. Of one thing we can be sure; of all the ages in which to suffer from a deficiency of confidence or an inferiority complex, this present one must be quite the worst. Sophisticated competition and expertise is all around us in today's technological world, and the appallingly high rate of psychotic illness and suicide is tragic proof of that.

To those who suffer from this personal setback, there is good news indeed. Christ can give you confidence in yourself if your confidence is placed in Him. He will give you resources within your own being which will make all the difference. Call to mind that time when Simon Peter was first introduced to the Saviour by his brother, Andrew. The Lord looked at him and read him instantly. "Thou art Simon the son of Jona," He said; "thou shalt be called Cephas, which is by interpretation, A stone" (John 1:42). Peter was not lacking in self-confidence, as we saw earlier, but he was deficient in spiritual adequacy; and the

Master saw him not as he was by nature, but in terms of what He could help him to be. "Thou art . . . thou shalt be"—that is His way for us, too.

The living water of the Spirit shall be, to the believer, a well of water "in him" (4:14)—an assured source of inward supply. Just to emphasize that this matter of the healing of one's personal deficiencies is intimately related to the life of spiritual victory, Jesus sought out the man whom He had healed and said to him afterwards, "Sin no more, lest a worse thing come unto thee" (5:14). His touch can take care of the problem.

3

His Touch and Sanctification

Sanctification begins at the new birth and ends in heaven. Its whole aim and object is the transformation of the lives of saved people after the pattern of the Saviour's own. As soon as we personally accept Christ and yield our lives to be His, we are, in that limited sense, sanctified; that is, separated from the old life and placed under His sole ownership. When our pilgrimage has ended and this mortal has put on immortality, we shall be finally sanctified, saved from the very presence of sin in any form or from ever being in contact with it again.

In between, there stretches a lifelong process of Christian nurture with, at some stage along the way, a catalyst leading into a deeper experience of grace in which we realise a purifying of the inner nature and experience more effective power for service and soul-winning. This personal upturn in the quality of our discipleship we call "entire sanctification"; entire, that is to say, not in the sense of completion or terminal satisfaction, but in the sense of entirely equipping us for our role as Christians in the family, in the church, and in the community. It leads to further, and indeed better, growth towards maturity and spiritual stature.

To many believers, sanctification has been understood in terms of personal excellence, superior zeal, and intensity of spiritual effort. These values, however, are rather the result of sanctification than the cause or essence of it. In itself, the experience is a fulness of love wrought in our hearts by faith in the Scripture promises of God. Paul's definitive exposition of entire sanctification in 1 Thess. 5:16-24 ends with the assurance, "Faithful is he that calleth you, who also will do it." Many similar statements in the Word of God could be cited, all showing that from first to last, it is a work of faith in which the Holy Spirit applies the precious blood of Christ to neutralise the stains of the heart and comes to abide in fulness so as to produce in clean soil the fruit of spiritual character. This appropriating faith is dependent for its operation on our total obedience to God's will as we understand it day by day and the willing compliance and cooperation of our will in all things as a settled commitment.

Just how central faith is to the core of Christian experience is demonstrated in the miracle of the healing of the centurion's paralysed and dying servant (Matt. 8:5-13; Luke 7:1-10). His master believed that it would not be necessary for the Lord actually to come and heal him personally (he felt too unworthy for such honoured attention, anyway) but that He had only to give the word and it would be so. Once he knew the Saviour was willing, faith would do the rest. No wonder Jesus said He had not found such faith before even among His own people, let alone Gentiles like this Roman officer.

Now the centurion would not have been a man in whom faith would come easily. The Romans were not used to believing in the unseen. Their god was the iron power of their imperial state, and their creed was essentially earthly and inflexibly logical. The almost mechanical operation of military discipline to which he referred was typical of the Roman mind. One can almost hear the click of heels in his words! Yet this officer believed that just as surely as obedience unquestioningly followed command, so Jesus could give the order for his servant to be healed without even having to be present by his sickbed.

> *Faith, mighty faith, the promise sees,*
> *And looks to God alone;*
> *Laughs at impossibilities,*
> *And cries, "It shall be done."*

Our inheritance as Christians is "among them which are sanctified by faith that is in me" (Acts 26:18). The Lord still responds to implicit trust. The faith that triumphs over signs, works, and human expectation is the faith that delights Him and brings spiritual wholeness to our souls.

Faith, however, has to cut its teeth and learn to endure. Mere easy-believism does not suffice. For proof of that, take the case of another man who came to the Lord and besought His help in a desperate situation—Jairus, the synagogue leader whose daughter lay at the point of death (see Mark 5:22-43; Luke 8:41-56). On the way to her bedside, the Master stopped to speak a word of comfort and assurance to a stricken woman who had reached out from the crowd and touched the hem of His robe. We can imagine how poor Jairus felt. Precious moments lost! And all for the sake of someone who had not even had the courage to come up openly and ask Jesus for help as he had done, and whose need was so much less pressing than his own. Surely, after 12 years, a few more minutes would not have mattered.

Indeed, the very thing he feared did happen. Friends came and told him that he need not now trouble the Master—his little girl was dead. Poor Jairus! We can see him turning a grief-stricken look to the great Healer whose aid he had so counted on and yet had now sought in vain. A word from Jesus, "Be not afraid, only believe," and they hurry on. Wonderful delay! Jairus asked the Lord for a healing, and he got a resurrection!

It is often that way. Delay is not desertion. Frequently it is divinely intended so that the answer, when received, shall be all the more wonderful because of intervening factors which we could not see but were foreknown by Him. Wellington waited feverishly for the Prussian General Blücher's promised arrival on the field of Waterloo to support him against the French; and as the fateful day wore on, it seemed as though Napoleon was gaining the upper hand. Four o'clock in the afternoon; the enemy was attacking more heavily than ever, and still no sign of the promised relief. Then, just as the battle seemed all but lost, a thunder of hoofs over the distant hills, a trumpet call; and on to the field of conflict swept the Prussians—late, but not too late! The hard-pressed British rallied, and the little emperor's hopes of European dominion vanished forever.

Does the Lord sometimes delay His response to the earnest believer's prayer for deliverance from inward sin and for the fulness of the Spirit? If the work is by faith, surely it must be ours as soon as faith rises in our hearts to embrace the promised blessing. Yet, despite this fact, we have known sincere seekers who have told us that they consecrated and believed over and over again but never received a clear assurance of being sanctified wholly, so that they almost despaired of such an experience being truly valid.

There have been reasons for this. "Ye ask, and receive not," said the apostle James, "because ye ask amiss" (4:3). Some Christians seek the blessing just for the power to serve, and thus unconsciously they may be ministering to their own pride. Others may seek just to please their pastor, parents, or spiritual friends, or out of a desire to sit on the church board and be numbered among the "best set" in the church. More often than not, however, the reason is not an unworthy one at all. It is simply that the seeker has not yet grasped the whole truth about his or her own need. Seeing oneself as God does can be pretty desperate work, and there is no shortcut through it.

That is why the Lord, though well able and abundantly willing, does not normally justify freely and sanctify wholly the soul at the same time. There is an interval so that with the new light of the new birth, we may see ourselves from a spiritual and not merely a natural standpoint. This may well be a very testing time, and discovering the depth of the problem may cause discouragement; but if we press through with unwavering trust, God will not fail.

When we have thus laid the groundwork of testing our motives in order to put our all honestly on the altar and have made our commitment to the holy life, the moment to exercise appropriating faith will come. It is as though a window is opened to the soul, and we are aware that this is God's "now" for us. It is a moment of promise and of opportunity, and it must be taken. Decisive faith is achieving faith. To sidestep it is to lose it. Like saintly John Fletcher of olden time, we must take a stand and declare, "I am dead indeed unto sin and alive unto God."

Two blind men were sitting by the roadside in the dusty way leading from Jericho to Jerusalem (Matt. 20:29-34). It was a busy road, and often a dangerous one, it seems; for on this route Jesus depicted the lonely rider being attacked and robbed and left lying helpless in the road until the Good Samaritan found him. Probably these blind beggars would be quite used to hearing commotions of one sort or another, but on this particular day there was a special air of excitement. Jesus of Nazareth was passing through!

If we are to judge by their immediate cries to Him to have mercy on their piteous condition, these men had heard of Jesus already. That would be hardly surprising. All sorts of talk and news of the day would reach their ears from the many travellers who passed them daily, and the wonderful healings and cures wrought by the Prophet from Galilee were being spread abroad throughout the land. Perhaps they had longed, and even prayed, that one day He might pass their way and restore their sight as He had to so many others like them (cf. 9:27-31). And now at last, their opportunity had come—here He was approaching! It was well that they seized it when they did, for He was to come that way no more. The Master was going up to Jerusalem to die.

Blind folk are very sensitive and quick to perceive "atmosphere"—it is part of the endowment of a kindly and merciful Providence to them—and these two seem to have sensed that this moment was not to be lost; for when the crowd bade them be quiet, they cried out all the more loudly, "Have mercy on us, O Lord, thou Son of David." Their cries were heard by the Saviour and their great need was gloriously met. Let the soul that is seeking holiness take its cue from them; as soon as the Lord gives the assurance that you are ready and He is waiting, close in at once and claim the blessing.

Two things need to be said about this sanctifying faith. First, it is not dependent on signs. When faith is firmly grounded upon the Word of God, it can sustain the new relationship without needing to be reassured or doubly convinced by any external phenomena. The Spirit gives the direct witness to the heart (Acts 15:8-9; Heb. 10:14-15), and the heart is content. We will experience the difference by the joy and peace and spiritual poise that we never knew before.

When the Lord Jesus returned to Cana, where that very first miracle had been performed, He met the nobleman with the sick son and once more was begged to go and save a soul from death (John 4:46-54). This was in Galilee, where He knew He would have a hard time convincing the people of His Messiahship by word of mouth; they were only interested, it seems, in the dramatic and breathtaking evidence which His miracles had afforded them. Hence His complaint, "Except ye see signs and wonders, ye will not believe" (v. 48). The healing was granted, but by word and not by touch; at a distance and not for all to see. Faith is vital; signs are only needed when the Lord has a special place for them in His plan and purpose.

This teaching is nowhere more important than in regard to the baptism with the Holy Spirit. Though accompanied by signs on the Day of Pentecost, it was even then essentially a faith experience, the result of the disciples' waiting for the promise of the Father in obedience and trust in its fulfilment. A personal Pentecost may perhaps be attended by some unusual confirmation today, as many will testify; but one of the chief errors of recent times is the idea, usually promoted with great enthusiasm, that there must be "initial evidence," by which is generally meant speaking in unknown tongues, to validate any real experience of the baptism of the Spirit. It will never be known how many earnest seekers after that experience have waited in vain for such manifestations and, when these have failed to appear, have given up the quest in despair and even in disgust.

The gifts of the Spirit are matters we must leave with the Spirit, whose work is "dividing to every man severally [individually] as he will" all that we need for the service He has planned for us to do (1 Cor. 12:11). Verses 4-11 make that position perfectly clear beyond all reasonable doubt.

The second pointer to the true nature of sanctifying faith is that it works by love. It ushers in a new dimension of devotional love for Jesus that, being free from the entanglements of other loves, is total towards Him. Ten lepers met Jesus; and in answer to their plea, He told them to go and show themselves to the priest as provided for in the Law (Lev. 14:1-2) in the case of a leper who claimed to be cured. They obeyed His instruction, went off in search of the priest, and were cleansed as they went. In other words, they had the right kind of faith—literally, obedience in action. But a word of further assurance and blessing awaited the one out of the group who thought enough of his Healer to return and thank Him for the deliverance he had found (Luke 17:11-19).

This gives us good reason to ask what part love and gratitude for the Giver plays in the soul's quest for wholeness. In fact, it plays a very large part. To hear of so great a salvation as that obtained for us at Calvary, and to bow low before the Redeemer, as this Samaritan did, in utter thankfulness and heartfelt appreciation for something so wonderful, is to be well on the way to finding its richest treasure; for deeply felt gratitude implies acceptance of the offer. There is a faith that believes "God can"; but there is a better faith that believes "He does" and thanks Him with an undying love. This is the true faith to which the Lord gladly responds with His comforting assurance.

Hester Ann Rogers, who as a religious but socially active young girl in Macclesfield, England, came under the influence of the early Methodist preachers and was truly converted, and whose writings were a guide to many seeking entire sanctification in the 18th century, thus expressed her own deeper experience of grace: "While lost in communion with my Saviour, He spake those words to my heart, 'All that I have is thine. I am Jesus, in Whom dwells all the fulness of the Godhead bodily. I am thine. My Spirit is thine. My Father is thine. They love thee as I love thee. The whole Deity is thine. He even now overshadows thee. He now covers thee with the cloud of His presence.' All this was so realised to my soul in a manner I cannot explain, that I sank down motionless, being unable to sustain the weight of His glorious presence and fulness of love."

Hester Ann's grateful acceptance of such a great love led her to find the inward enjoyment of its fulness. This may well be the way for some of us to enter this new dimension of Christian life.

Earlier it was written that the exercise of this decisive faith for full salvation represents a second crisis in the unfolding pattern of personal salvation, one which opens the way to accelerated and richer progress in Christian living. Many question this and urge upon us the idea that spiritual nurture involves only growth, with perhaps a bridgehead regarding consecration on our part but nothing more.

The fact that a second touch from the Lord is needed to bring the soul into the fulness of the blessing is illustrated in two other of our Lord's miracles. These do not stand alone as types or symbols in the abstract but answer to such an experience in the lives of Abraham, Jacob,

Moses, Gideon, Saul, David, Elisha, the first disciples, the Samaritan converts, Cornelius and his family, the apostle Paul, the Ephesian believers, all of whom received a crucial work of grace after they had already known the Lord.

In restoring the sight of the blind man at Bethsaida, the Master's first touch upon his eyes brought him partial sight (Mark 8:22-26). He was able to see "men as trees, walking." He was no longer blind but could see only imperfectly. The second touch brought him perfect vision. So it is with the soul. To be converted is to be no longer blind; being born again, we can now see the kingdom of God, but we have not yet fully seen ourselves nor yet apprehended all that Christ can do for us. We are so far babes in Christ; and like an infant in natural life, although possessed of sound eyesight, we do not understand all that we see. God gives to us according to our faith; and when we discovered our guilt as sinners and sought pardon and release from that burden, He gave us through Christ the assurance that we had passed from death unto life.

But going on with the Lord brought us fresh revelations. We found within ourselves some things that appalled us: pride, for example; selfishness; vain ambition; weakness of the flesh in many areas; and inner spiritual defeats. We only saw them with the new vision of renewed life. Thus it is that to the deeper need not known before, Christ reveals himself to us in His second touch as the One who saves to the uttermost those who come unto God by Him. When we accept this, we are ushered into the fulness of fellowship and freedom; and like this blind man, we can go forth with full vision, full assurance, and a clear witness of victory. The hymn writers have given us words which are probably sung more than they are heeded: "Be of sin the double cure; / Cleanse me from its

guilt and power"; "Let us see Thy great salvation / Perfectly restored in Thee." It is the second touch that does it!

When you come to think of it, life in its fulness never
comes all at once. The child becomes the man or woman.
The bud becomes a fully opened blossom. The life in
the seed germinating below ground becomes the life of the
plant growing above the soil. The chrysalis becomes the
butterfly and the fledgling the airborne bird. There is a
point of breakthrough in each case, just as there was in the
case of Lazarus (John 11:43-44). He came forth from his
tomb of death possessed of all the essentials of reborn
life—breath, movement, responsiveness to sound and
name. But he was bound—hand, foot, and face—with the
evidences of his former state. Full resurrection life came
with the liberating command of the Lord Jesus, "Loose
him, and let him go." Every conversion is a resurrection,
but the newborn soul is still limited in its enjoyment of the
new life which it has in Christ by the lingering shades of
the old life.

Love of the world, old habits curbed but yet un-
broken, attitudes of mind and heart formed over the years
of sin-life and self-life that still assert their mastery—these
arc the graveclothes that bind the soul of a Christian until
we allow the Saviour to strip them off and lead us into
fulness of life in Him. It was He indeed who said, "I am
come that they might have life, and that they might have it
more abundantly" (10:10).

The second crisis is not the last that we shall know in
our pilgrimage, and the blessing then known will be the
first of many more if we follow on with the Lord. All that
we have been will not become all that we hope to be over-
night or even in a few months or years. But there is a point

in Christian experience beyond conversion when we must submit to full release in a definite surrender and step of faith that does represent, in John Wesley's famous term, "the Second Blessing, properly so-called."

4

His Touch and Stress

When you consider that the humanity of our Lord was as total as our own, it is wonderful to see how He could handle stress. Of the fact of His vulnerability to it there can be no doubt. The incessant demands on His patience and energy must often have reduced Him to the point of exhaustion. The Gospels reveal little of it, to be sure, but the glimpses we get here and there of a weary Saviour tell their own story. For all that, His outbursts, when they came, were always controlled and necessary, never in the least impatient or fretful.

Unlike the three areas of Christian concern we have been considering so far, this matter of stress is one in which His need and ours exactly correspond, because He "was in all points tempted like as we are, yet without sin" (Heb. 4:15). He was no less a human being because He lived on earth as the Son of God. It may help us to find His touch upon our stresses and strains if we first take a look at the way in which He reacted to a sudden emergency, an episode that might well typify the many tight moments that come our way, often with devastating results.

It was a storm at sea, one of those short but quite vicious ones that often break over the Sea of Galilee on account of its topographical location (Matt. 8:23-27; Mark 4:35-41). Jesus and the disciples were riding in a small boat when the storm struck and seemed likely to overwhelm them. Sometimes our stressful moments come suddenly like that, when we are least expecting them; or at others we are exposed to prolonged pressures such as, to quote the hymn writer, "when sorrows like sea billows roll."

Now the really significant point of this incident is not so much that the Lord rebuked the wind and calmed the sea. After all, He who brought the elements into being and ordered the natural laws under which they operate, is well able to control them at His will. Even by nature, storms do sometimes cease of their own accord quite suddenly; and in an instance of this on the coast of Kent that I can recall, the effect was quite uncanny. One minute, the trees were almost bending under the force of the gale; the next, they were upright again, the wind had dropped almost to nothing, and a gentle drizzle was falling. So while not doubting for a moment that He did indeed subdue the storm, there is obviously more in the miracle for us to see.

Surely the detail that we are chiefly meant to notice is that Christ was asleep in the midst of the storm. Mark records that He was asleep on a pillow. He had not just nodded off for a few moments; the tired Saviour was probably sleeping soundly, thereby showing that it is gloriously possible to be perfectly at rest inwardly while the storms of life are going on all around. "Let the peace of God rule in your hearts," Paul told the Colossians (3:15);

and how sorely do we Christians need this inner tranquility so as to be kept in perfect peace whatever the circumstances. That is the answer to the problem of stress, but finding it has sometimes proved a baffling business. It often seems as though our difficulties are calculated to dishearten and exasperate us, and there is no escaping them. Can we find spiritual release for such times as these?

Take the case of the Syro-Phoenician woman who pleaded with Jesus to heal her afflicted daughter (Matt. 15:21-28; Mark 7:24-30). One of her nationality would be a worshipper of Astarte or the sun god, and her coming to the Saviour for help was an admission that none was forthcoming from her own deity. In her distraction, she sought the help of the Healer who "could not be hid," but the response she received was not exactly encouraging. "He answered her not a word." Then as she persisted, the disciples around Him tried to turn her away, and finally came the crowning rebuff: "I am not sent but unto the lost sheep of the house of Israel." The Lord had a certain way of bringing His redemptive purposes to pass: "To the Jew first, and also to the Gentile" (cf. Rom. 1:16). It is ever so; the purposes of God unfold and we are perplexed. What is the secret of victory in such circumstances? Not mere resignation to the apparently unavoidable, for the woman did not give up when told that she was not the immediate object of grace.

The secret is cooperation with the will of God, inscrutable though it may be; in coming to see that, in the divine economy, even stress has its place. This woman did not argue the point that others were preferred before her; she continued to plead in spite of it. She saw beyond the present extremity: "Yes, Lord: yet the dogs under the table eat of the children's crumbs." One day, her people would be admitted to the kingdom of God. Likewise, we must look to Him in simple faith to remember us in our present burden while at the same time fitting it into His overall plan. In this way, we may find strength to go on, and the same kind of dignified poise that this anxious woman displayed. Her faith was rewarded and the prayer granted. Dependence, cooperation, and confidence are a trinity of attitudes that always win through in the end.

The supreme stress, without question, is bereavement; and it all too often finds us quite unprepared for it. The raising of the widow's son at Nain reveals the Lord's great compassion towards those who mourn; because we can sense at once that the miracle was not wrought so much for the young man's sake as that of his mother, who felt his loss so bitterly (Luke 7:11-15). It was chiefly for her that the Lord had such a mighty sympathy. He knew her need; she was a widow and this was her only son and means of support in a hard world. Her desolation was doubly hard to bear. In a different way, perhaps, but no less certainly, Christ can transfigure the numbing darkness of that hour with His light and love. In the valley of the shadow, we need fear no evil.

But we must turn our thoughts in another direction, though a related one. In the Sermon on the Mount, Jesus said, "Blessed are they that mourn: for they shall be comforted" (Matt. 5:4). While this is wonderfully true of natural mourning, it really refers to a spiritual state. His evident compassion in the face of the one serves but to make us all the more assured of His tender concern and power to undertake for us during times of spiritual stress. These can vary: sometimes there is an acute sense of need when one is convicted of indwelling sin and is seeking deliverance; or it may be the realisation of our slow progress in the Christian life and of our personal unworthiness, to say nothing of times of actual failure. This is the kind of "mourning" to which Paul refers in 2 Cor. 7:7. It is not introspection or negative depression, but honesty before God. Distress over the sins of others and agonizing for revival and the salvation of souls is also a very real experience among the saints.

In any and all of these conditions, if the heart be genuinely broken, the Lord stands ready to perform a miracle! A cleansed and love-filled heart is a miracle and it is the result of spiritual mourning. A complete dedication and desire for service is a miracle of grace that will have stemmed from confession of our complacency and short-coming. The salvation of sinners and genuine revival in the church are the greatest of all miracles and cost the prayer agony of faithful souls. When Catherine Booth was asked to advise in a desperate case where everything seemed to fail, she replied, "Try tears." Mourning leads to miracles!

The composer Joseph Haydn, when court musician to an Austrian prince whose estates lay deep in the country, was asked by his players to obtain leave for them to go to Vienna to visit their wives and families, whom they had not seen for months. The prince would not hear of it, so Haydn hit on a plan to make him change his mind. He wrote a symphony—his No. 45, the *Farewell*—in the finale of which each orchestral part came to an abrupt end, leaving only one violinist still playing at the end. When it was performed, Haydn instructed each player that when his part ended, he was to pick up his music, snuff out his candle, and leave the platform. When the solitary violinist finished, he was to do the same. The astonished prince, at first infuriated, later saw the message in the music and granted the request. Haydn worked a miracle for his men because he understood their distress and cared enough for them. Our Saviour will work miracles for us if only we will get distressed enough over the need for them.

Soul rest and inner poise in the face of stress is not a matter of detachment or even discipline, but of decision to make use of available resources. "There remaineth therefore a rest [margin, 'a keeping of a sabbath'] unto the people of God" (Heb. 4:9). What a beautiful provision God has made in the Sabbath day of rest and worship; let us cherish it and keep it always! Similarly, we need to observe the soul sabbath whereby we are released from a code of religious works into the glorious freedom of appropriating faith. Everything we need for spiritual completeness is provided for us in the atonement of the Lord Jesus Christ and the gift of the Spirit.

The Lord did indeed use miracles for the very purpose of drawing attention to the true nature of the day of rest. One of these was the healing of the man with dropsy whom He found among the people gathered in a Pharisee's house to which the Master came for a Sabbath day meal (Luke 14:1-6). They were watching Him to see what He would do; and the whole episode might very well have been staged for Him as a trap by the Pharisees themselves. He openly challenged them, nevertheless: "Is it lawful to heal on the sabbath day?" They made no reply and the man was healed.

That this holy day has a God-given sanction for all men, and for Christians most especially, is of course implicit in the teaching aroused by this miracle; but the essence of the Sabbath is more even than this. The physical rest from everyday employment has a spiritual counterpart in the rest of soul which is to be found in Jesus. In Matt. 11:28-29, the rest He offers to responsive souls is followed by the second rest available to yielded disciples. The first is a rest from the burden of sin, the second a rest from the tyranny of turmoil. He takes the other end of the yoke and so keeps us steady and undismayed.

The old Swedish saint, Arvid Gradin, whose testimony so charmed John Wesley when he visited the

Moravian community at Herrnhut in Germany in June, 1738, spoke of his experience of sanctifying grace as "repose in the blood of Christ . . . and a cessation of all, even inward, sins." The Son of God is truly Lord of the Sabbath both for the body and the soul; indeed, for the entire personality. What John Wesley called, theologically, the second blessing, his brother Charles, poetically, called the second rest. Hear him ardently sing:

> *To me the rest of faith impart,*
> *The Sabbath of Thy love.*

The negative grace of heart cleansing is matched by the positive grace "to help in time of need" (Heb. 4:16), so that stress is cared for just as fully as sin is dealt with. When all has been said about the pressures of daily life, which Christians are called upon to face no less than other people, the ultimate conclusion we must reach is that God's way is the only way and that acceptance is far better than resistance. Our comfort and strength is that "all things work together for good to them that love God, to them who are the called according to his purpose" (Rom. 8:28). Remember, Satan can contrive nothing which the Lord does not first allow in order to lead us to greater victories of His grace.

All four Gospels tell of the incident in the Garden of Gethsemane when Peter drew a sword and cut off the right ear of Malchus, the high priest's servant, who was among the group sent to arrest Jesus. Only John, however, gives the names of the two men, and only Luke adds the significant information that the Lord at once healed the severed ear (22:50-51). Even in the hour of His capture, He "went about doing good." What miracle could teach us more than one wrought at such a time?

The Lord reminded Peter that He did not need swordplay to defend Him; a host of angels could do that far better by His merely breathing a prayer to His Father for help. But neither sword nor angels were needed just then, for there was a cup to be drunk to the full—the cup of human iniquity—and the Lord Jesus did not flinch from it. The way He had to go was the Calvary way, and there was no other way that could achieve the desired result, the redemption of mankind.

If that redemption is to be fully accomplished *in* us as it has been *for* us, then it is just as true that God's way is the only way. Neither human effort, no matter how well intentioned (like Peter's sword), nor divine intervention in the sovereign process of human decision can suffice for the work of remaking lives. God's way is the way of the Cross. Part of the package called holiness is the ability to cope with crisis the Calvary way. To the Galatians who were trying to make themselves perfect through fleshly effort, Paul testified, "I am crucified with Christ: nevertheless I live; yet not I, but Christ liveth in me: and the life which I now live in the flesh I live by the faith of the Son of God, who loved me, and gave himself for me" (Gal. 2:20). The inward emancipation from both sin and stress is realised by Christ's indwelling by His Spirit, and the way to experience this is the way of the Cross.

The English Methodist preacher, Mark Guy Pearse, described his own spiritual pilgrimage in lyrical vein. Having listened to several discouraging arguments against his ever finding the object of his quest, he remembered how well he had fared previously on the holy hill called Calvary. So he went forth again and climbed until he reached the top and could gaze again upon the Saviour. He was surprised to see Holiness sitting there at the Master's feet; and as he felt again the greatness of His love to him, "Holiness rose up and came to me all graciously, and said, 'I have been waiting for thee ever since thy first coming.' 'Waiting there?' I asked, wondering. 'At His feet,' answered Holiness; 'I am always there.' "

That is God's way for us, too, and it is the only way. It leads from the vale of tears to the heights of holy vision. Let's try it!

5

His Touch and Service

Christian service, whether full-time or lay, is in essence Christian witness. Its most distinctive, even definitive, form is preaching, which is really public witness to Christ by proclamation of the gospel. But Christian workers do other things, too; things that other people also do, such as teaching, nursing, practicing medicine, and caring for the handicapped and deprived. The only difference is that Christian involvement in the social sciences carries an additional objective not sought by other agencies, and that is to make known by these means the love of God and the living reality of Christ in such a way that the good rendered to mankind may lead to spiritual experience and not merely the betterment of the people.

Christian service is therefore Christian witness. No

less so is a layperson's daily occupation in the community or in industry and the professions. It is all for the purpose, not simply of earning a living or serving one's generation, but of making Him known whom the world so desperately needs.

There may be those who would say, "It is enough to love people for Jesus without necessarily talking about Him," and who would therefore relegate witnessing to the minister or missionary and such other Christian folk as may have a particular gift for it or simply possess extrovertive natures. There can be no doubt that this is a terrible mistake. The risen Lord promised the disciples (all of them) who were assembled on Mount Olivet before He ascended that when they were baptized in the Spirit, they would be witnesses unto Him, beginning right there in Jerusalem and reaching out to the far corners of the earth. They would not all be apostles or evangelists, but they would all be witnesses, and the record of the Book of Acts is that "the Word of God grew and multiplied" (Acts 12:24). Their lives certainly witnessed for Christ, but not without the spoken word.

Spiritual power for Christian service, then, is inescapably tied in with personal testimony to saving and sanctifying grace. The Holy Spirit is given to believers with the prime intention of equipping them for this very thing. Holiness is service-oriented just as much as it is related to the inner spiritual life. This is seen in its most luminous form in the miracle involving the woman suffering from hemorrhage who unintentionally interrupted the Master's journey by reaching out to touch the hem of His robe as He passed on His way to the home of Jairus to save his little daughter. He knew that virtue had gone out of Him and stopped to ask who had touched Him, much to the surprise of His companions who formed quite a crowd around Him. The woman then acknowledged to the Lord that it was she who had done so, told Him all about herself, and testified to the wonderful healing she had received (Mark 5:24-34).

All who have written on this tender and gracious miracle have very rightly seen spiritual as well as just physical healing enshrined in it. The woman's trouble was loss of blood, and that means she was losing her very life. The interests of the soul were at stake, and she needed life both physical and spiritual. Sin's disease and nature's disease alike are dispelled by Him "whose touch has still its ancient power." Sin is a deep-seated malady of the soul, and as such needs both pardon and cleansing— justification and sanctification—if salvation is to be complete. Jesus himself pronounced the woman whole, and we know that health and holiness have a common origin in experience as well as in the root word from which both are derived.

Now there are two points of great significance about this. First, the woman sought and found her cure furtively, and the fact was only known to the Lord. Just so are our dealings with Him over salvation and holiness; they concern only us and Him, and no one else need be involved at all. But the second point is that she could not keep quiet about it! Even though she would rather have kept it to herself for reasons of womanly modesty or natural reserve, she was obliged to testify before the people as to what the Lord had done for her, like the Spirit-filled disciples who insisted to their persecutors, "We cannot but speak the things which we have seen and heard" (Acts 4:20). It is hard to resist that kind of testimony!

Personal witness was obviously the keynote of the Early Church's astonishing progress and rapid growth. Likewise, it was the power behind early Methodism and the old-time Holiness Movement. In these crucial days, people seem very open to talk about spiritual things and willing to listen to the Christian message. The tensions of the times and the reaction against affluence and widespread materialism have set many seeking for something better and more enduring. The fringe churches and quasi-Christian groups have moved into this vacuum with devastating success. We must move into it, too, with the vitality of a true Bible-based avowal of full salvation; we must tell those ready to listen how Christ can deal with sin at the source and how the Holy Spirit can give peace, poise, and power to overcome the pull of the world.

One of Satan's master strokes is to keep Christian people silent and so rob the world of hearing the Good News at first hand from living witnesses while at the same time depriving the believer of the joys of soul-winning. We can see this tyranny in the case of the dumb spirit which the Lord cast out of more than one man who was specifically declared to be "possessed with a devil" (Matt. 9:32-34; Luke 11:14-22). The demon kept him dumb when God wanted him to speak and designed his vocal cords to that end. The enemy, with his usual arrogance, sought to effectively silence what the Lord had tuned for His praise.

While no one will deny the power of a life quietly lived for Christ even when little is said about salvation, it is still true that very often verbal testimony is held back when it should be given. "Be ready always to give an answer to every man that asketh you a reason of the hope that is in you with meekness and fear" (1 Pet. 3:15). That is the New Testament standard for witnessing, and it especially applies to those who by nature are not bold or assertive. God is ready to help the shy and hesitant—indeed, He often puts a special attraction upon their words; but the embarrassed silence, the half-ashamed confession of Christ, or, more often, the change of subject when personal religion comes up in conversation, have frequently cut off what might have been a fruitful introduction of someone to the Saviour. There is such a thing as the sin of silence.

I have a newspaper clip about an elderly and infirm woman living alone in a London basement who one day was found dead in bed. A diary was found near her, which she had kept up right to the day of her death. Day after day, the only entry was "No one came." Her very life had depended upon someone to drop in each day, if only for a few minutes; but no one came until it was too late. How many souls are eternally lost each day because nobody cares enough to tell them of the Saviour?

This whole question really brings into the arena the bitter, implacable hatred and militant opposition of Satan to the kingdom of Jesus Christ. Wesley used to say that perfect love was the doctrine that God especially blessed and the devil particularly hated, simply because Spirit-filled Christians were making such colossal inroads into his kingdom of darkness. The strength of this opposition is seen very starkly in the angry and quite unprovoked outburst of the unclean spirit which infested the man in the synagogue at Capernaum. The demon spoke for all the cohorts of evil: "What have we to do with thee, thou Jesus of Nazareth? art thou come to destroy us?" (Mark 1:24; Luke 4:34). Yes, praise be! He had. The Son of God was not only "manifested to take away our sins" but also to "destroy the works of the devil" (1 John 3:5, 8).

Let any Christian mean business with God and dedicate all to the Lord's service, and he or she will become a prime target of the devil and will experience countless pitfalls and snares and baleful temptations such as could scarcely have been conceived possible. The holy walk, with all its joy and peace, is not a no-go area for the enemy and is anything but immune from his astute attacks. This very fact led one writer to pen this line:

"They who fain would serve Him best are conscious most of wrong within," which has unfortunately discouraged so many from seeking to be sanctified wholly. Those words have made it seem impossible.

It certainly is true that earnest seekers after the blessing will feel quite sinful at times, and the devil will see to it that they get so disheartened, they will give up the quest, but this idea is not true of those who, in humble trust and loving obedience, open their hearts to the Holy Spirit to be cleansed and filled. They will be conscious most of a wonderful release and an enduement of power they did not know before. The conflict with evil will certainly always be going on, but it will be external and not in the inner life while we walk with the Lord.

Are we seeing that happen in our service for God? Sadly, not always. We have a problem of powerlessness. The fact is, the enemy is getting too much of his own way; and we sometimes look here, there, and everywhere for the cause when we might find it within ourselves. Take, as proof of this, the pathetic case of the father who brought his epileptic son to the disciples in the hope of having him healed of his disorder. The Master was absent, having taken Peter, James, and John up into a mountain to pray. It was there that He was transfigured before them. When they came down from the mount, the Lord and these three were confronted with this unhappy scene—the distraught father, the frenzied lad, and the embarrassed disciples standing by helplessly.

Undoubtedly it was a hard case. To begin with, the parent himself was lacking in faith. Jesus countered his "If thou canst do" with a firm "If thou canst believe" (Mark 9:22-23). How very different was this man from the four friends of the paralytic, the Roman centurion with the sick servant, and the Syro-Phoenician woman seeking healing for her daughter; these, by their simple expectation of an immediate response to their need, drew forth His praise. Not so this man! He was a part of the "faithless and perverse generation" which so burdened the Lord by its stubborn unbelief (Luke 9:41). There was a want of faith, too, on the part of the powerless disciples. Why, one cannot think. They had cast out unclean spirits before in the Master's absence and came back from their missions glowing with reports of the wonderful things that had happened under their ministry.

The clue to the problem lies in the Lord's final words to them, "Howbeit this kind goeth not out but by prayer and fasting" (Matt. 17:21). The ordinary, commonplace situation can be met with an average amount of faith; but special cases like this, where the power of Satan is particularly virulent and there are background problems adding to the difficulty, can only be overcome by special faith which can only be generated and released by prayer and fasting. By whom? By those directly concerned with the situation. There was a prayer meeting actually going on while these frustrated healers were vainly trying to grapple with the case before them—a prayer meeting in which the very glory of the Lord had shone forth; but even this did not alter the course of events down there in the valley below.

One has only to glance through the well-known incidents in the Acts of the Apostles to see the effect of the baptism of the Holy Spirit in the prayer life of those saints. Those who previously could not watch one hour with their suffering Lord in the Garden of Gethsemane could now pray all night (perhaps for many nights) for Peter's release from prison. No wonder the angel turnkey was dispatched to open his cell! Samuel Chadwick, the great English

Methodist preacher, said many times that chief among the benefits he experienced from the baptism of the Spirit which he received in 1882 was that it taught him to pray, and this it was that revolutionised his ministry.

Akin to the problem of powerlessness is that of fruitlessness. Nonproductivity in Christian discipleship has always been a major setback in the postapostolic Church. When Jesus came to the fig tree standing beside the road from Bethany into Jerusalem, He found only foliage on it; there was no fruit. Hardly surprising, you may think, since the time for figs to appear had not yet arrived. Why, then, did He expect to find any, and pronounce the sentence that withered the tree on account of its absence? (See Matt. 21:18-22; Mark 11:12-14, 20-24.) The Master undoubtedly had Israel very much in mind, for the best that she could produce was the foliage of Pharisaism—luxuriant, but lacking! Yet because she had the knowledge of the true and living God, Israel could and should have produced the fruit of love to God and man which other nations, in their pagan ignorance, could not be expected to show. Hence the demand for figs when by nature, none could be looked for. God works in His people along the line of the supernatural, not the merely earthly.

But this principle is not only national; it is also personal. Jesus turned to the disciples who were with Him and said, "If ye have faith . . . ye shall . . . do . . . " It is simply because heart holiness is the true mainspring of fruit bearing in the Christian life that it is essentially a faith experience and produces the fruit of Christlikeness and effective service where otherwise this would not be possible. The growth that took place in the Early Church after Pentecost is proof enough of this fact; and Peter's reference to the events recorded in the second chapter of Acts in his report to the church in Jerusalem on the mini-Pentecost in the home of Cornelius (Acts 15:8-9) makes it abundantly clear that God gave them the "witness, . . . even as he did unto us; . . . purifying their hearts by faith." Whether Jew or Gentile, the Spirit-filled Christian can bear fruit under any circumstances.

So faith and fruit go together. The saintly life is nurtured on appropriating faith which enables the believer to love and to trust, to endure and achieve, to sing and to shine in conditions where nature alone could not survive, let alone overcome. Charles Wesley's hymn puts it so well:

> *All things are possible to God,*
> *To Christ, the power of God in man,*
> *To me, when I am all renewed,*
> *When I in Christ am formed again,*
> *And witness, from all sin set free,*
> *All things are possible to me.*

But how can barrenness be turned to fruitfulness? Well, let us join Simon Peter and his fellow fishermen as they speak with the Master on the lakeside shore after their unsuccessful night's fishing. In the fresh morning light, He uses their boat as a makeshift pulpit to teach the people, and then tells Peter to launch the boat again and let down the nets for another catch. The disciple protests that it will do no good after their disappointing night's work; but all the same, he proceeds to do as the Master said, at least to the extent of letting down one net. Even with that incomplete obedience, they bring in a catch so huge that it nearly sinks the boat (Luke 5:1-11)!

This was to happen again, as recorded in John 21:1-6; and when it did, Peter must have remembered that previous time when he and the others had left all to follow Jesus. "Launch out into the deep," He had then said; and when they saw the miraculous draught of fish, they hesitated no longer but launched themselves out to follow the Lord in total commitment.

But in that grey and cheerless morning three and a half years later, when the same trio with some other disciples were again returning from a night of fishing with empty nets, and the risen but unrecognised Lord stood on the shore, He called to them across the water a very pertinent question, "Children, have ye any meat?" The word really meant "relish" or "extra delicacy"—that something special that turns a meal into a banquet. No wonder there came back the dismal "No" in reply. There are indeed many Christian lives whose discipleship has lost its relish. The sparkle; the wonder; the sheer, luxuriant joy of the Lord have given way to a rather mechanical routine: prayer without much praise, Bible study with little excitement, witnessing that is correct but no longer compelling. How sad!

It is perhaps significant that the miracle recorded in Luke 5 took place not at the first introduction of the fishermen to Jesus and their beginning to follow Him, for that had already happened as told earlier in the Gospels; but it marked their later step of entire devotion to Him to the exclusion of all else. In other words, it brought about that consecration which only one already acquainted with the Saviour and enjoying His fellowship can make, and from which all true Christian service must spring. This is how we become fishers of men.

The fact that the miracle was, in substance, repeated by the risen Lord, when the call to service was renewed and the disciples had faced the implications of Calvary and the Resurrection, underlines the very vital point that the consecration made when seeking the fulness of the Spirit needs to be renewed at each later development of spiritual understanding and encounter. Having "launched out" to claim the promise of sanctification, we must "cast the nets" again and again in updated dedication and yieldedness. Consecration and faith are not static things.

They are continuous, progressive, and expanding values. We keep the blessing just as we first obtained it, by launching out on His Word. Failure to do this leads to loss of spiritual relish and ineffective service.

*   *   *

The last word must now be said and it really brings us round full circle to where we began. Christian service is Christian witness, even when expressed in terms of practical ministries. Jesus needed to emphasize in His day—and still does in ours—that showing love for people in everyday things was all-important to Him. The Pharisees complained when He shared a meal with tax collectors and sinners and when He, with the disciples, ate some new-plucked corn and healed sick people on the Sabbath day. On both counts, He returned them the same answer by quoting Hos. 6:6, "For I desired mercy, and not sacrifice" (Matt. 9:13; 12:7). Religious duty without concern for man and beast was not a true interpretation of the will of God. Just as in the case where He had healed the man with dropsy, the Lord also defied the scribal limitations of the Sabbath by healing the man with the withered right hand actually during a synagogue service (Matt. 12:10-13; Luke 6:6-10).

Perhaps we need to reevaluate our understanding of the implications of perfect love. We are often so deeply (and rightly) concerned about maintaining our standards and safeguarding evangelical tradition that we fail to show the love of God to people as people and not simply as "souls." We may feel that we are called only to be "spiritual" and that we can well leave the works of charity and social concern to the state or the churches that preach a social gospel. But the truth is that perfect love is at once the most spiritual and the most practical religion there is. It sees an opportunity for evangelism in everything!

62

Even before his "warmed heart" experience in Aldersgate Street, John Wesley, already hot in pursuit of holiness, led his little group of Holy Club members into the gaols and alleyways of Oxford to help the prisoners and the poor. When the great Methodist Revival was sweeping Britain, he administered homely cures for diseases, tramped the streets in search of coals and blankets for destitute folk, and lent his pen to the war against slavery and other abuses of human rights. Following in the same stream of holiness evangelism, General Booth saw that the way out for darkest England in the 1890s lay not only in preaching the gospel of full salvation but also in feeding the hungry, sheltering the homeless, and lifting those who had fallen in the battle of life. Likewise, Phineas Bresee knew that he could not preach holiness in plush-lined pulpits and leave skid row untouched in downtown Los Angeles.

Holiness leads to helpfulness. It did so in the earthly life of our Lord. It did so in the life of the Early Church. It has done so in every sphere of genuine revival through the annals of church history. It must not fail to do so today. Jesus said, "The poor always ye have with you" (John 12:8); and everywhere, all the time, there are people who look to us as Christians in their times of need which are not always purely spiritual. Let us demonstrate to them the true nature of perfect love. Our touch is His touch when we reach out the hand of friendship and concern.